· MEET ·
PIERRE-AUGUSTE RENOIR

Read With You Center for
Excellence in STEAM Education

Read With You

ISBN: 979-8-88618-088-6
First Edition January 2022

Vase of Roses, c. 1890–1900

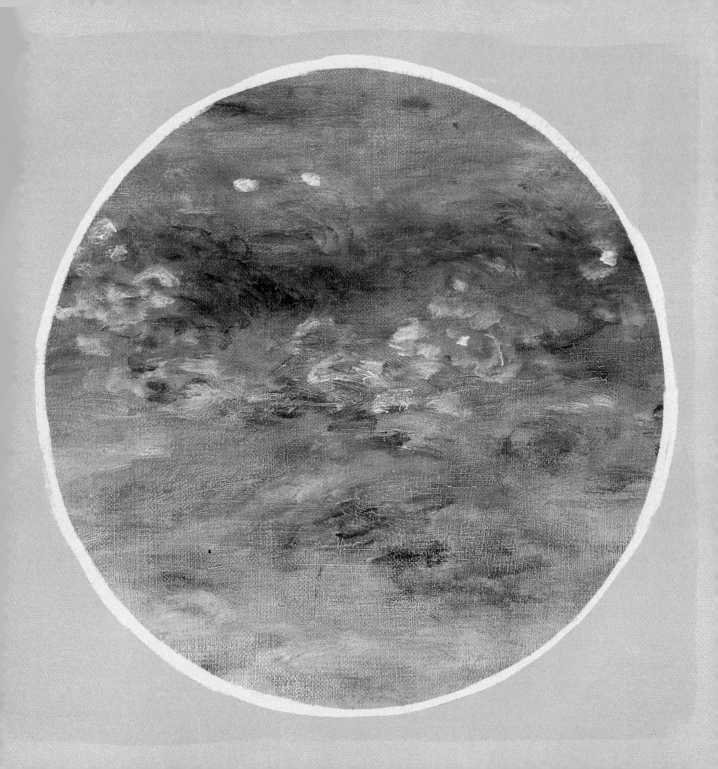

Landscape, 1900–1905

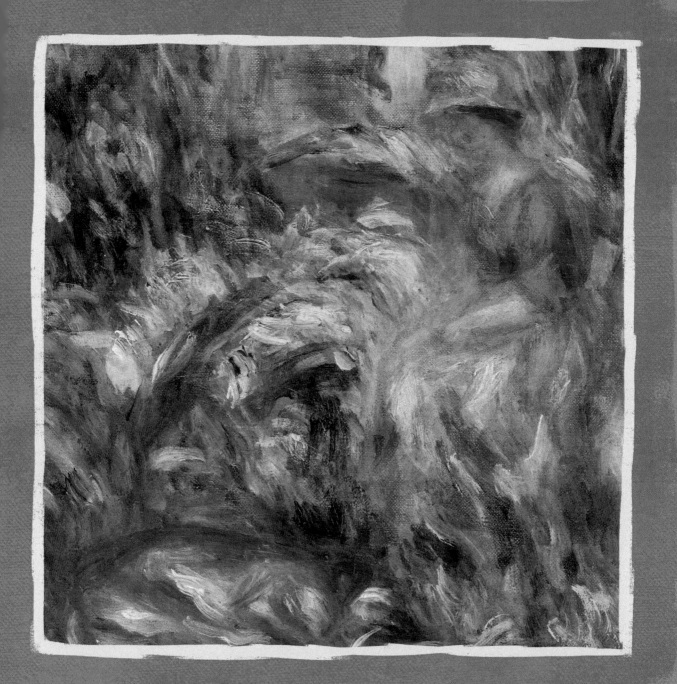

Farmhouse, 1917

Landscape with Figures, near Cagnes, 1910

Picnic, 1893

Landscape, 1911

Two Women in a Landscape, 1918

Near the Lake, 1879

Find Examples

This painting is titled *Seated Woman with Sea in the Distance* (1917). It is in Renoir's famous Impressionist style.

What colors does he use most for his paintings?

Do the colors look like happy colors or sad colors?

Since the woman is drawn very simply, what things did Renoir add so people would know she is a woman?

Renoir always wanted his paintings to bring happiness. Do you think he succeeded?

Connect

This painting is titled *Claude Monet* (1872). Claude Monet was another famous Impressionist painter and a good friend of Pierre-Auguste Renoir. He often painted outside with Renoir.

This is one of Renoir's early paintings. Compare it with the other paintings in this book. How are his colors and brushstrokes different here?

What do you think Renoir felt about his friend, Monet?

Which of your friends likes to draw?

If you drew a picture of them, what would it look like?

Craft

Option 1

1. Take some paper, an easel, and watercolor paints outside to the most beautiful place you can find.

2. Using the watercolors and simple brushstrokes, paint your impression of that place.

3. Use bright colors and wispy brushstrokes, like Renoir.

Option 2

1. Lay tracing paper over your favorite Renoir painting and trace a person or object in the painting.

2. Cut brightly colored paper into small random shapes.

3. Using a glue stick, glue the paper shapes onto the tracing paper outline to create a cutout version of Renoir's painting. It's impossible to mix colors this way, so they will be unmixed, like Renoir's colors!

Made in the USA
Las Vegas, NV
12 February 2024

85676584R00024